THE RUNAWAY

Robert Frost

Illustrations by Glenna Lang

David R. Godine · Publisher · Boston

For my first best friend, Ellie Frost,

and for our daughters,

Arielle Frost Hinckley & Esmé Lang von Hoffman

First published in 1998 by
David R. Godine, Publisher, Inc.
Box 450
Jaffrey, New Hampshire 03452

Library of Congress Cataloging in Publication Data
Frost, Robert, 1874-1963.
The runaway / Robert Frost ; illustrations by Glenna Lang.
p.   cm.
Summary: A poem about a colt frightened by falling snow.
1. Horses—Juvenile poetry. 2. Children's poetry, American.
[1. Horses—Poetry. 2. American poetry.] I. Lang, Glenna, ill. II. Title
PS3511.R94R86   1996
811'.52—DC20   96–13267 CIP

ISBN 1-56792-006-3

First printing, 1998
Printed in Hong Kong by South China Printing Co.

THE RUNAWAY

Once when the snow of the year was beginning to fall,

We stopped by a mountain pasture to say, "Whose colt?"

A little Morgan had one forefoot on the wall,

The other curled at his breast. He dipped his head

And snorted at us. And then he had to bolt.

We heard the miniature thunder where he fled,

And we saw him, or thought we saw him, dim and gray,
Like a shadow against the curtain of falling flakes.

"I think the little fellow's afraid of the snow.
He isn't winter-broken. It isn't play

With the little fellow at all. He's running away.

I doubt if even his mother could tell him, 'Sakes,
It's only weather.' He'd think she didn't know!

Where is his mother? He can't be out alone."

And now he comes again with clatter of stone,
And mounts the wall again with whited eyes

And all his tail that isn't hair up straight.
He shudders his coat as if to throw off flies.

"Whoever it is that leaves him out so late,
When other creatures have gone to stall and bin,

Ought to be told to come and take him in."

Robert Frost (1874-1963), the most admired American poet of the twentieth century, wrote "The Runaway" while teaching at Amherst College in western Massachusetts. It first appeared in the *Amherst Monthly* in June 1918 and was recognized by faculty and students as a metaphor suggesting the impetuous spirit of youth. But "The Runaway" is also a charming nature poem about a young colt confused and skittish at the sight of his first snow storm. A poet whose verse is often more complex and profound than it appears on first reading, Frost frequently intended different layers of meaning.

Although born in San Francisco, Frost spent most of his life in New England, whose old farms and woods inspired much of his poetry. Frost graduated from high school in the Massachusetts mill town of Lawrence as co-valedictorian with Elinor White, whom he later married. Although he attended two New England colleges, Dartmouth and Harvard, he never acquired a degree. As he found his calling as a poet in New England, Frost taught school (following in his mother's footsteps), worked as a reporter, and tried his hand at poultry farming. "The Runaway" is set in a rocky New England mountain pasture and describes a Morgan horse, a sturdy breed developed and still popular in Vermont.

Frost first achieved recognition as a poet in England, where he moved with Elinor and their four children in 1912. There he found a publisher for his first two books of poems. When he returned to America three years later, his poetry was eagerly sought by editors who had previously rejected his work, and he became a professor of literature. He won the first of his four Pulitzer Prizes in 1923 for a collection of verse called *New Hampshire,* in which "The Runaway" appeared. In his later years, Frost became America's unofficial poet laureate. He was the first poet invited to read at a presidential inauguration where he gave his moving rendition of "The Gift Outright" for President Kennedy in 1961.